Social Media Marketing

Strategies for Beginners to Use Facebook, Youtube, Twitter, LinkedIn, Snapchat and Pinterest for their Business

© Copyright 2017 by Dan Healy. All rights reserved.

ISBN-13: 979-8617772120

In no way is it legal to reproduce, duplicate, or transmit any part of this document in either electronic means or in printed format. Recording of this publication is strictly prohibited and any storage of this document is not allowed unless with written permission from the publisher. All rights reserved.

The information provided herein is stated to be truthful and consistent, in that any liability, in terms of inattention or otherwise, by any usage or abuse of any policies, processes, or directions contained within is the solitary and utter responsibility of the recipient reader. Under no circumstances will any legal responsibility or blame be held against the author or publisher for any reparation, damages, or monetary loss due to the information herein, either directly or indirectly.

Respective authors own all copyrights not held by the publisher.

Legal Notice
This book is copyright protected. This is only for personal use. You cannot amend, distribute, sell, use, quote or paraphrase any part or the content within this book without the consent of the author or copyright owner. Legal action will be pursued if this is breached.

Disclaimer Notice
Please note the information contained within this document is for educational and entertainment purposes only. Every attempt has been made to provide accurate, up to date, and reliable complete information. No warranties of any kind are expressed or implied. Readers acknowledge that the author is not engaging in the rendering of legal, financial, medical or professional advice.

By reading this document, the reader agrees that under no circumstances are the author or publisher responsible for any losses, direct or indirect, which are incurred as a result of the use of information contained within this document, including, but not limited to errors, omissions, or inaccuracies.

Trademarks

The trademarks that are used are without any consent, and the publication of the trademark is without permission or backing by the trademark owner. All trademarks and brands within this book are for clarification purposes only, and are owned by the owners themselves, who are not affiliated with this document.

Table of Contents

Introduction 1

1. Some General Advice Before Starting 2
   Resources 2
   Smart investment 3
   Display patience 3
   Networking 4

2. Facebook 5
   Page visibility 6
   Posting visibility 6
   Targeting and privacy for posts 6
   Messages 6
   Country restrictions 6
   Personality 7
   Consistency 7
   Frequency 8
   Business Goals 8
   Facebook Advertising 9

3. YouTube 10
   Setting It Up 10
   Videos 11
   A Good Thumbnail 11
   Use Trends 11
   Annotations 11
   Promote On Other Channels 12
   Captions 12
   Miscellaneous 12

4. Twitter 14
   Know what you want 14
   Basic Set-Up Tips 14
   Why? 15
   Engagement 15

- Creativity 16
- Get Noticed 16
- Being Consistent 16
- Hashtags 17
- Be Professional 17
- Help Others 17
- Tweet Statistics 18
- Follow 18

5. LinkedIn 19
- Creating A Page 19
- More Information 20
- Audience Engagement 20
- Other Tips 21

6. Snapchat 24
- Sales 24
- Snap-Stories 24
- Workplace 24
- Consistency 25
- Geo-filters 25
- Sponsored Posts 25
- Contests! 25

7. Pinterest 27
- Linking Back 27
- The Right Pins 27
- Verification 27
- Manage Your Boards 28
- Rich Pins 28
- Engagement 28

8. Blogging and SEO 29
- Blogging 29
  - Business blog 29
  - Guidance 29
  - Reviews 30
- Search Engine Optimization (SEO) 31

What to do next: Take Action! 32

Introduction

In the last few years, social media platforms have been the most happening places. Naturally, with everything going online, businesses couldn't have been left far behind.

It had been only months since people had accepted the idea of being online-social that businesses started emerging and hogging the limelight across various platforms. It, therefore, comes as no wonder that almost all businesses that run offline also have an online presence.

Man is a *social animal*. With the advent of technology, he has gradually learned the art of online-socialization. In this book, 'Social Media Marketing', I will unlock the doors to expanding your business beyond its offline potential.

This book is written with the sole intention of familiarizing you with the idea of social media marketing for your business. It primarily covers Facebook, YouTube, Snapchat, Twitter, Pinterest and LinkedIn and how you – a beginner – can utilize these platforms to not only reach out to your customers, but also make new ones.

Since the book is written to be read in about an hour, you will soon have a great stepping stone upon which to build the foundations of a successful marketing campaign for your business.

Let's get started and dive straight in!

1. Some General Advice Before Starting

Jumping into Social Media Marketing can be daunting, but with good planning and preparation, you will be in a confident position to take your business forward to the next level. Below is a collection of aspects to bear in mind before you get started with the different platforms, and some general advice on setting your expectations for progress at the outset. As with many things, investment of time and energy upfront will yield dividends in the end, but it can take time for social media to work its magic, depending on what you hope to achieve for your business.

Resources

Most online businesses start from scratch, but it would not hurt for you to have a financial backup put in place well in advance. Moneymaking is a dicey business, especially so when it is online. A few wrong decisions and you could lose the fortune of your lifetime. All your investments stand the risk of crumbling up in smoke all because it is the Internet and there are no rules.

At times, it becomes challenging to regulate things as neatly as you would like things to be controlled in real life. Despite the presence of cyber laws, Internet thieves manage to find a way out to dupe people of stores of money. Therefore, it is wise to keep aside a certain sum of resource aside for emergency circumstances.

Smart investment

It is the rule of any business that you should not put all your eggs in one basket. It just means that you are not a good businessman if you invest everything in one place. Just because it is online does not mean it is safe from threats and takeovers. Before you know it, your website could be hijacked by Internet thieves and hackers.

Do not make the horrible mistake of putting all your life savings on the web. Be smart enough to distribute your money equally among at least three different places of business.

Display patience

Just because it is the Internet and everything except the Internet connection is free, does not mean that everything does happen at the click of a mouse. Remember, though online, it is still a business and businesses do not build themselves all overnight. Do not expect results when you start out. In fact, you should expect some negative feedback. Underestimating yourself is the best way to prepare for failure.

However, do not overdo it. Coming back to the original point, exercise some patience. It is only by being patient that you will learn how success can be achieved only through hard work.

If online businesses involved no hard work, everyone would be doing it. They come with their share of toil and must be done diligently.

Networking

The importance of a good network in an online business, or any business for that matter, cannot be directly put into words. Networking merely means that you have a real web of contacts that could come handy to you at various stages of your business. It means that you, as a businessman, should have enough people on your contact list.

Networking is vital for your business to spread. Customer attraction is a major part of any business. When you are done finalizing your product, manufacturing it, and doing all the associated works that come with it, it is time for you to start talking about your work. The more you talk about your business, the more people come to know about it. This 'talking' can be done by advertising it. Now anyone can call uptake agency and put in an advertisement for their product.

However, mere advertising is not enough in most cases. No one notices the billboard sitting idly at the side of the road. Even if they do, it gets brushed off as just another advertisement. However, you could be smart about spreading the word about your work. This is the Internet, and you are an astute businessman; do not forget that.

2. Facebook

Everyone is on Facebook these days. Most businesses that have a Facebook page of their own are observed to be experiencing a lot more footfall than those who don't. Creating a Facebook page is not rocket science. Follow the given steps to make one.

The very first step is to log onto Facebook.com and click on the 'Create A Page' button present at the bottom. It will be easy if you already have a Facebook account as you can easily create a page by signing into your existing account. Alternatively, you can enter Facebook.com/pages and create a page. Once done, you can enter the name of the page.

Remember to take your time and not rush the decision. It is best to consult with friends and family before coming up with a name for the page. Facebook allows just one change of name once the page has been created.
Once done, you can click on the type of business you own. You will have to choose one from the following options.

- Local business or place
- Entertainment (promotion)
- Brand or Product
- Company, Organization or Institution
- Artist, Band or Public Figure
- Cause or Community

You can now fill in the 'About' info details before adding your website's address. Once done, Facebook will give you your unique URL for your page. Next, you can choose the preferred page audience; for instance, if you have content for people above 18 years of age, then you have to specify it to your audience.

If you are not yet ready with your page, then go to the settings and edit the page visibility and choose "Unpublish page" to continue editing the page without being disturbed.

Here are the different page elements you can choose...

Page visibility
Here you can choose who can view your page. If you are keen on making it a private page, then you can modify the settings and make it a closed group

Posting visibility
Here you can choose who can post on your page. Sometimes it's important to limit the posts so that you don't end up with a page consisting of a million posts.

Targeting and privacy for posts
This is to capture a particular audience. It is important to aim the posts to a certain audience, so you send the message across to the right audience.

Messages
These are the messages that your page can receive. If you are taking orders from people through your Facebook profile, then you can create filters to keep the spam at bay.

Country restrictions
People from specific countries can view your page. Sometimes it's best to limit the page to only those countries where your business operates, so you don't receive spam.

Personality

It is quite important for you to add a certain personality to your Facebook page. People should be drawn to it and feel the urge to like or comment on the page. If you settle for something mediocre, then it will not work in your favor. The good idea is to hire professionals who are good at molding pages and making them interesting for the audience. You have to instruct them to review the audience and prepare an analysis of their general characters. Doing so helps in developing a fitting schedule that will make your page popular.

You can also look at the strategies that some of the other companies are employing and come up with a plan that is in keeping with the same. However, it is best to maintain a little originality and remain true to your company's policies.

It pays to have a good sense of who you are and what your company stands for. If you remain confused, then it will go against you. It is best to work out an image that you would like to portray and then pursue the same. Remember that things can look like one thing in your mind and another thing on paper. So it is best to create a page and check if it looks exactly like you planned it.

Consistency

Remember that consistency is key. You have to be consistent with your posts, and they should be coherent. Your Facebook page should be a slice of your store and the products you sell there. Don't make it too different as it can confuse your customers. If you have a team working for you, then instruct them to post the posts at regular intervals and not keep the audience waiting.

A good trick is to know when people prefer to have an update come their way and give it to them. But don't make it boring, as you have to keep your audiences engaged. Again, you can look at a successful company's strategy and come up with a posting schedule that suits your own business. As mentioned earlier, it is best to aim for the early evening slot, as that's when most people are active on email.

Frequency

When it comes to maintaining an online profile for your company, it is essential to be as frequent as possible. You must try to post new posts at regular intervals so that people know what to expect and when to expect them. A golden rule is to post in the evenings, as that is when most people expect new posts. Try to increase the frequency of the posts as and when the company grows.

Some companies prefer to post new posts thrice a day as that helps in keeping the audiences glued. But it is important not to get carried away and post too many things all at once. You cannot overload the audience with too much information, as it will end up confusing them. Keep the information relevant and coherent. You can always do a short trial and error to see what is working for you and what isn't.

Business Goals

It is quite important to be in sync with your business goals and update your page from time to time by keeping in mind the primary motives. Your page should be an exact representation of your company's motives. Your page should speak of your ambitions. It should portray your true intentions. It pays to incorporate a little of your company's policies in every new post.

Facebook Advertising

Facebook advertising is a potent tool that you can use to promote your products and services. Advertising on Facebook is straightforward once you know how to go about the process. Here is how you can get started with it. Once you have your ad permit, go to the "manage your ads" button on facebook.com/adsmanage. Once you are there, pick the options; you would like to incorporate in your ads feature. If you wish to create an ad from scratch, then here are the steps to follow:

- **Choose the type of ad** that you wish to control. This depends on what you want the ad to stand for.
- Next, **choose the objective** of your campaign and incorporate it in the ad as extensively as possible.
- **Select the demographic** that the ad will be displayed too. Doing so will help your ad connect better with the chosen audience.
- **Pick a budget** that you wish to allow for the ad. It pays to have a number in mind as it helps you stay on track and prevents overspending. You can set the budget based on how big you want the ad to be.
- Lastly, you must **create an audience** for your ads. You should keep in mind the audience that will be viewing your ads and incorporate elements that will please them.

3. YouTube

YouTube has grown into an influential social media platform. What started out as a fun medium of introducing the world to three-dimensional interaction has now turned into a powerful tool of marketing.

Just like in every other social media channel, the secret to success is getting a following or audience to broadcast your videos to. The more views you get, the more popular your videos will be and the greater success you will have in ranking highly in the search results. Here are some tips to get you started when creating and promoting your YouTube channel.

Setting It Up

When creating your YouTube channel, ensure that you use your company's name and any relevant branding resources to make sure that your channel is easily identifiable to your target audience. Also, ensure that you have a clear, catchy and straightforward company description.

Look for ways of linking your YouTube channel to your other social media pages to provide cross promotion. You can also do cross promotion through linking your channel to other pages that you are affiliated with. When you start, the next step is to promote your channel to ensure that you get the most views on your videos.

Here are some tips to get more views...

Videos

Videos that subtly attract people to click on them when they show up in the search results. In this case, you should strive to shoot and upload all your videos in HD format. As such, you must ensure that your videos are shot in an environment with perfect lighting. You don't have to do hours of video to pass your message across. More people are likely to watch short videos than extremely long ones so keep that in mind when creating videos.

A Good Thumbnail

To be honest, most of us only click on YouTube videos that already seem to be descriptive of what we are looking for. We mostly judge this by looking at the thumbnail. Therefore, ensure that you have one that is highly captivating to maximize clicks to your channel.

Use Trends

Although you shouldn't be misleading in your titles, using hot titles will increase your chances of attracting an audience through organic search. This works similarly with the thumbnail. A catchy thumbnail can enhance the number of views on your videos to a large extent.

Annotations

You can interlink YouTube videos through annotations (these can appear at the top left and at the top right corner of each video whereby the ones at the bottom link to the previous video while the ones at the top link to the next video). You can use annotations to develop a menu screen at the end of each video whereby the viewer is presented with other videos that he or she can choose from. With this option, it will be a lot easier for people to navigate between all your videos, which in turn result in more views.

Additionally, you can use annotations to point users to a playlist or the page that prompts the viewers to subscribe to your channel.

Promote On Other Channels

Share your YouTube videos on other social media sites like Twitter and Facebook. Whenever you upload a video, share it with your networks and ask your friends to share it or like it as well. Ensure that each video has a clear call to action asking viewers to subscribe or share the videos. You can opt to use this in the middle or at the end of the video.

Captions

If you don't want to lock out people who have hearing problems, you can use captions in your YouTube videos (captions are simply the YouTube's subtitles). These captions also come in handy for those who want to watch videos without turning on their volume. Additionally, the content is also searchable on YouTube's search, which in turn means you will find it easier to rank. To add captions, click edit a video then choose the captions tab.

Miscellaneous

Ensure that you have a consistent pattern of uploading new videos to your YouTube channel. This predictability is very critical if you want to have a dedicated following. Ensure that you engage your followers always by responding to comments, suggestions and other forms of feedback from your audience. Your responses should be prompt. Partner with bloggers within your niche. These would probably be willing to share high quality and informative videos on their blogs. With this option, you will generate more leads, more views, and more subscribers. You will also have a valuable backlink to your video. Having your video embedded in a page with a high page rank increases your chances of ranking highly on YouTube. You might need to give them an incentive to promote your video on their blog. You can as well have a blog that features the video.

4. Twitter

Twitter is the second largest social media site after Facebook with over 280 million monthly users and up to 500 million tweets sent daily. This is a huge market to market your products, but the challenge is; how do you do that with just 140 characters per tweet? How do you use the famous hashtags and other features that Twitter provides users to drive traffic to your blog, website or other social media sites? Here are some actionable tips to help you get the most from Twitter.

Know what you want

You can only understand the nature of the information that you will be tweeting if you know what you want. Are you a blogger wishing to share ideas and content about what you write about or do you simply want to be sharing news or following celebrities? When you know your purpose, you will be tweeting on relevant topics.

Basic Set-Up Tips

- Make the Twitter handle (name) the **same as your other** Social Media application's page names.
- Make sure your profile has **keywords**. This will make it easier for people to search you on Twitter. You should also publish your Twitter handle on other platforms simply to attract a new following.
- **Provide all the required and relevant information** while creating your Twitter account, as it will make people more aware of your business.

- **Avoid using special characters and punctuations** so that users will be able to reach your website with ease.
- **Customize your Twitter profile** to make it more interactive and attractive. Make it look more like you. Your goal is to develop a social media brand so try to use the same branding features you have on your Facebook profile on Twitter.

Why?

Ensure that you give your audience some form of the incentive of why they should follow you. For instance, you could offer exclusive access to something that your audience would be interested in. Post regular offers and promotions for stuff that your audience finds amazing.

Engagement

Follow people or businesses that you consider necessary based on the industry they are in and the kind of things they tweet about. Go on to favorite tweets, retweet tweets, and respond to tweets. This works in that people will start listening to you when they notice that you are acknowledging or listening to them.

Likewise, if anyone follows you or even mentions you on Twitter, you should try to respond to them and even thank them. Retweet any great content that you find. You will realize that more people will start engaging you when you engage them. Look for weekly chats and participate in the conversations. In this case, engage them with hashtags but ensure that you don't overuse them. Also, ensure that you don't use hashtags that could easily make your content end up being grouped with inappropriate content.

Creativity

Be creative in your content creation; use the 140 characters you have at your disposal to craft captivating tweets. In some instances, you might need to retweet other people's tweets or content unlike creating your content. As you do that, ensure that you keep in mind why you are doing it, who is your target audience and what you hope to achieve through that.

Get Noticed

Learn to use pictures to pass a hundred words as opposed to relying on the 140 characters at your disposal. Use inline images in your tweets to generate more followers. As you do that, use images that speak positively about your brand. You will notice that tweets with images have more favorites and retweets. According to the Twitter Media Blog, posts that have images attract over 30% more engagement than the standard tweets.

Therefore, it is clear that you should be relentless in your image creation. Share infographics that explain some complex concepts in simple and few words. In doing so, you are bound to have far more engagement than constantly tweeting empty (with no image) tweets.

Being Consistent

Consistency is key in any social media marketing effort. You can do so through creating tweets that are in line with your brand's tone, mission, and vision. Ensure that your voice is unique and active on Twitter.

Also, ensure that you are consistent with as far as timing for Twitter is concerned. If you are usually active on Twitter on specific days, be active on those days. You could even automate the tweeting process to ensure that you don't miss an important moment to tweet. This will make your followers expect something from you during those days, which can ultimately grow your audience.

Hashtags

You can ride on a trending hashtag to promote your business. Just check the popular tags and figure out how you can add value to the conversation while ensuring that you support your business. Try to offer an attractive deal to get guys to like your page.

Be Professional

You should experiment with tweeting at different times to learn when best to engage your audience because they are listening. Also, there is a limit on the number of times you should probably tweet; you can only know that when you experiment. You could also schedule your tweets and monitor notifications to ensure that you have an organized way of doing things.

Help Others

If you know something that someone else might not know, don't be afraid to tweet about that. You will be amazed by the level of positive response that you will get from those who find your tweet very helpful. The rule of thumb is that you ought to treat others how you would want them to treat you if the roles were reversed. If you would sometimes want someone to help you on something, don't just withhold information that you know can help that person.

Just like in blogging, don't be afraid to share it all because this will pay back in multiples. For instance, if you are attending a conference, which is bound to attract people who don't live in your city, you could tweet about the best hotels, best restaurants, best cab services, best night out joints, fun things to do in your area and many other things. The more help you give, the more people feel as if they are indebted to you. They will always stop by to check out what you have been up to.

Tweet Statistics

It is very easy to click on a tweet that has figures on it than one that seems to provide an opinion on something. Giving stats simply makes you have more credibility whatever you are tweeting about. This way, you stand a better chance of attracting people who are looking for hard facts about the subject.

Follow

It's a give-and-take world; more so in the Twitter-verse. When you follow others, they tend to follow you back, unless they happen to be some extremely popular personality. However, only by following others and their works, you will be able to gain a substantial amount of your followers.

5. LinkedIn

LinkedIn is next only to Facebook and Twitter when it comes to a customer base with over 200 million users. This implies a strong social media presence of business when it subscribes to the site. LinkedIn, as the name itself suggests, is about establishing and expanding your network. You must keep in mind certain figures before you dive into the site.

Almost more than half of LinkedIn's users are in the 30-50 age group. The website also boasts of a strong student presence. More than two-third of the LinkedIn users earn a hefty sum due to their businesses having a strong profile on the site.

The best part about LinkedIn is that it is strictly professional. You won't find users posting snaps of their latest party nights. Due to this, there is a lot of cutting to the chase happening. It provides you a no-bullshit approach to business.

You could go about creating and maintaining a LinkedIn profile in the following ways...

Creating A Page

You will have to first create a LinkedIn profile. This place is where you will be engaging your followers by posting news, events, content and other updates. You will be amazed that having a LinkedIn page will also help you rank higher in the search engines. Research has already shown that up to half of the members of LinkedIn are likely to buy from the companies that usually subscribe themselves on LinkedIn.

Once you create a page, you need to optimize that page so that it can show whatever your company offers. You could even build a products and services page on your page to attract more people. Ensure that you are very convincing on why people should follow you. LinkedIn company pages are also highly SEO friendly; Google even shows a preview of up to one hundred and fifty-six characters, so you need to have a compelling description that captivates everyone. Use relevant keywords as well. Don't forget to have your company's contact information, and any other information relating to your areas of expertise in this page. After doing that, ensure that you ask your customers to endorse your products or services.

More Information

People want to know whom they are interacting with on LinkedIn. The system is set in a way that makes it hard to find connections when you haven't filled your profile. As such, upload a good photo or logo of your company and complete every entry until your profile is completed. You can also post previous jobs or projects on the page just to show your credibility.

Audience Engagement

Try to engage the traffic as much as possible through responding to member comments. Ensure that you interact with people in corporate blogs, company posts and product updates to ensure that you always keep knowledge of your company in people's minds. Also, ensure that you customize content to your customer or follower's professional interests since this resonates with them. You can do that through sharing your content to all followers or a specific targeted audience based on the level of seniority, company size, industry or geography. Targeted engagement is a must have if you are to succeed in LinkedIn.

Always ensure that your posts start with catchy introductions and headlines; keep in mind that the audience won't read your posts if they don't find them captivating. Also, ensure that you keep your titles short. Nonetheless, you can always experiment to find out what works for you. The audience determines what is interesting by a simple overview of the first two or three sentences so ensure that you start on a high note.

Additionally, keep in mind that questions don't make good or captivating titles on LinkedIn. Also, ensure that your content is of high value to your readers by ensuring that you write something easy to consume and easy to share. This, in essence, should include such things like pictures, charts, articles, videos, etc. You could also ask questions to engage your audience more.

Other Tips

1. **Add a LinkedIn button to your website** and even use it in your email and blogs signature. This should ensure that it is easy for other LinkedIn members to follow you in a single click.
2. **Set up a custom URL**. Simply click edit profile then click edit. After doing that, check into the right bar on an option for customizing your URL.
3. **Send updates** about job openings to your connections. Also, search and answer various questions on LinkedIn and join groups that you can participate in. You could even create your group to discuss different issues of interest to your audience.

4. **Promote your LinkedIn page on other social media accounts** to drive traffic to your page. For instance, connecting your LinkedIn profile with your Twitter account can be a good idea. One way of setting up your account for that is to auto post your tweets in your LinkedIn status. Another good way is to choose to send tweets that have a #in hashtag to your LinkedIn profile. This ensures that you keep your profile clean and professional.
5. **LinkedIn users who consume professional content** usually spend about 8 hours every week reading about industry trends and news. You can leverage the power of LinkedIn publishing to grow an audience. You should ideally create posts that are between 1900-2000 words since this has been proven to attract more shares, views, and comments. You should as well post regularly and engage your audience consistently if you want to grow a large readership. Here are some more tips on success with LinkedIn publishing.
6. **Think of a middle school audience**: Don't write posts that are too complicated for people to comprehend. Even if the audience is largely an educated lot, most people still want to read posts written in an easy to understand writing style. These attract more shares, views, and comments.
7. **Don't be too opinionated**. Try to jog people's minds instead of providing a good or bad opinion about an issue of interest. Back your points with data if you want to come out as an authority in your profession.
8. **Use images**. As I have been insisting, an image speaks 1000 words so use it to capture people's attention and attract engagement. You should ideally

use eight images to attract the maximum engagement regarding shares, comments, and views for each of your posts. Videos don't add much value to engagement.

6. Snapchat

If LinkedIn is for strictly professional individuals, Snapchat is its polar opposite. What started out as a fun-filled website, has propelled itself into a major social media marketing platform in a couple of years. Before the big boom, it used to be a place for food enthusiasts and travel junkies. Now almost half of its users are directly or indirectly related to business.

Sales

Start with putting discounts and sale offers. When your Snapchat profile has exciting offers on sale, it is going to attract more customers. It goes without saying that the more the traffic, the better it is for your business. You can always put up attractive discounts and alluring offers.

Snap-Stories

Some of your offers could include something along the lines of "Post a Snap-Story of our product and avail 15% discount on its purchase". A snap story's life is 24 hours. It would not hurt customers to dedicate 24 hours of their life to a product they are interested in buying. This way, you could publicize yourself and make sales at the same time!

Workplace

Project your workplace environment to be a chill place. Arrange for couches and beanbags and make Snap stories out of your workplace. It has been observed that companies that post about their working conditions tend to have a lot of followers on social media platforms. When you connect to the masses in a way that is personal and relatable to them, it speaks a lot about how you want to reach out to them.

Consistency

You have to a regular to keep the numbers ticking. If you post only once a week, your followers won't feel connected to you. Make sure that you end up making at least 3-4 posts every day. Keep the frequency in check though. You would not want to spam the timelines of your religious fans. Today, businesses have legit vacancies for social media profile manager.

These are certain occupations that get salaries and incentives like a regular job. Companies are getting more aware of the importance and significance of a social media presence. You can always put up advertisements for such openings at your place.

Geo-filters

Snapchat has come up with different idea – Geo-filters. If you pay a nominal amount, Snapchat will allow you to create a filter of your own. You could make a unique screen that will speak about your business in its funny way. This filter will be available to only those people who happen to be within a limited geographical area. It is also a time-bound feature; so it's available for only a given period.

Sponsored Posts

There are many Snapchat Influencers who have a huge fan following. These influencers usually take some payment to promote businesses. Identify and single out such influencers that you think have the potential to reach out to consumers relevant to your products or services.

Contests!

You can hold Snapchat contests wherein you ask your fans to send you selfies or short videos with the product they bought from you. This may sound absurd, but it's a good marketing strategy. You may wonder, "Why should I engage with already present customers?" The answer is simple- because you need more. When fans send you their selfies or short videos, their friends get to see how they happen to be a loyal follower of you. This leads to a mass influx of new followers through your already existing fan-base.

7. Pinterest

An interesting phenomenon these days is the emergence of pictures as tools of mass media. A picture, they say, speaks a thousand words. This is truer in today's world as sites like Pinterest thrive on the same concept. An image-centric website, Pinterest started garnering traffic a bit late. Usually seen as the favorite place for newly-weds and travel enthusiasts, Pinterest is slowly expanding and encroaching upon areas previously dominated by LinkedIn and Facebook.

Linking Back

Never upload pictures of your business directly from your computer. Make sure you always link your pictures from your actual site of business. It serves two purposes; firstly, it leads your Pinterest followers to your original site, and secondly, it assures them of your authenticity. This method of leading followers to another site by way of indirect photo uploading is called linking back. You create a pathway for people to walk on and reach the target destination.

The Right Pins

Making a pin to an entirely irrelevant category is not only unhelpful but also counterproductive. When you put the wrong pins, it breaks your followers' trust in you. They tend to avoid following you and in extreme cases even unsubscribe. Make sure the pins you are using are accurately placed.

Verification

Once you verify your original website on your Pinterest account, it works wonders. It says a lot about how organized a business you are. It instills trust in your followers in the sense that they know where the content is coming from and who owns it.

Manage Your Boards

Optimize your boards according to your business. The description segment of your boards must be well filled. Although it allows you 500 words, make sure you wrap it up within 200 only. Keeping it brief and crisp actually, pulls a lot of fan following. Make sure that your board has a catchy name. The name should also speak something about what fans could expect it. Use words that are generic and will help you lead fans into your boards.

Rich Pins

Rich Pins are such pins that take users to a different website- usually the mother website of the business. They happen to be of six types currently-movie, app, product, recipe, article, and place. The best part about a Rich Pin is that it makes it clear from the very start that it will lead the user to a particular site. It does not mislead him or her in any way.

Engagement

Pinterest being a primarily image-oriented website does not allow for much interaction as opposed to sites like Facebook and Twitter. However, it does provide you options for fan engagement in the form of comments, likes, re-likes, pinning/repining, etc. Be genuine-sounding while interacting with your audience. Like their contributions or suggestions from time to time and try to incorporate the same into your website; this generates in them a feel-good emotion from being engaged with your business.

8. Blogging and SEO

Blogging

Words are said to be more powerful than swords and bullets. Words, when employed cleverly, could win you not just money but also wars and countries. Such is the power of words alone that they are said to be one of the most influential factors in any transaction. Why should your business be deprived of the blessing that is words?

Business blog

Start a blog about your business. A business blog is usually a place where you not only advertise your products and services but also attract customers via the same. A blog could provide all or any of the following kind of information:

- The **description of the exact products and services** your online business has got to offer. This blog could use the power of creativity to make sure that not only are your customers informed but attracted as well.
- The **pros and cons** of a particular product or service. Your blog is supposed to be a platform where the general public gets to know about the unbiased opinions about your business. Do not always praise and boast about your successes. Admit defeats by warning your customers against some slip up you might have made.

Guidance

The best form of help you can provide via a blog is guiding your clients regarding any queries they might have about a product or a service. Open a hotline number that is to be managed by an employee the entire day. Any aggrieved or curious person can contact this number in case he's got a complaint or curiosity.

Reviews
Invite people to give reviews about your business. If you have worked decently so far and your business has been in the market for a fair amount of time, people are bound to have liked your service. Why refrain from exploiting their satisfaction to further gain in the popularity sector? Allow people to leave star ratings and valuable feedback by including a box for feedback on your website.

Your blog need not necessarily about your business alone. It could be about the general market as well. You could review other businesses and the entire market if you have the time, thereby establishing a good platform for customers to come and get honest views not just from consumers but also from an established business person, which will be you.

Blogging is a great way to make sure that your business reaches out to people and because everything is online, you do not have to sweat it out in the sun hanging posters and running for billboard authorities. Hire a good web designer who could set up a well-maintained website for you to operate.

Make sure you are well acquainted with the functions of all the features of the blog and your website. Do not write just for the sake of it; write so as to keep the average customer informed and entertained. Your graph keeps going up as long as you are regular with your blog. When you are irregular, people lose interest after a while, and that affects your credibility as a businessman since they cannot trust you to deliver on time and at a uniform frequency. Moreover, they also lose out on getting updated with the recent developments in the product or service they have subscribed to or bought from you.

These days anyone who has an internet connection has got a blog of his own and does not require any official publication to let people know his or her views on things ranging from life issues to scientific ones. Starting a blog is a great booster to your online venture.

Search Engine Optimization (SEO)

Have you ever tried to Google a particular entity? If yes, then you must be aware of how Google shows you results, yes? Say if you typed in the search bar "Tiger", it would show you all possible results related, remotely or otherwise, to the animal tiger. However, if there has been recently a warship named 'Tiger,' and the same has caused ripples in the social media world, then this piece of news is going to appear before any other. Have you ever thought as to why the results are arranged in the way they are arranged? The answer is Search Engine Optimization.

The idea is very simple. When you write about your products or services, you have to be as simple as a worker bee. You cannot afford to clutter your blogs with contents that have very little to do with what the core of your business is or is supposed to be. Be precise while talking about your product. If you have an associated website to your online business, make sure its content does not beat around the bush and do not contain matter that is irrelevant to the fundamental principles of your business. Search Engine Optimization is a great way to regulate, which search appears first and which one appears last when an innocent consumer decides to find out about your merits on the Internet.

What to do next: Take Action!

I hope that this concise look into the world of *Social Media Marketing* has whet your appetite for more, and has ignited an enthusiasm in you to take the next step and implement some of the ideas here for your business.

Fundamentally, what makes you different from your competitors is *your willingness to engage* with your customers personally, allowing them a peek into how your business is run and making them feel connected to your products or services. *Social media marketing has made all of it possible.*

Online business marketing is not rocket science, and this book has explained why.

I hope you had a good time reading it and have lots of practical tips to get you on your way to more success on the web.

And finally... If you liked the book, please consider leaving a review on Amazon.

Thank you very much!

www.ingramcontent.com/pod-product-compliance
Lightning Source LLC
Chambersburg PA
CBHW050306220526
45465CB00002B/851